Bella,
the Wildlife Ambassador
Protecting Piping Plovers
Third Edition

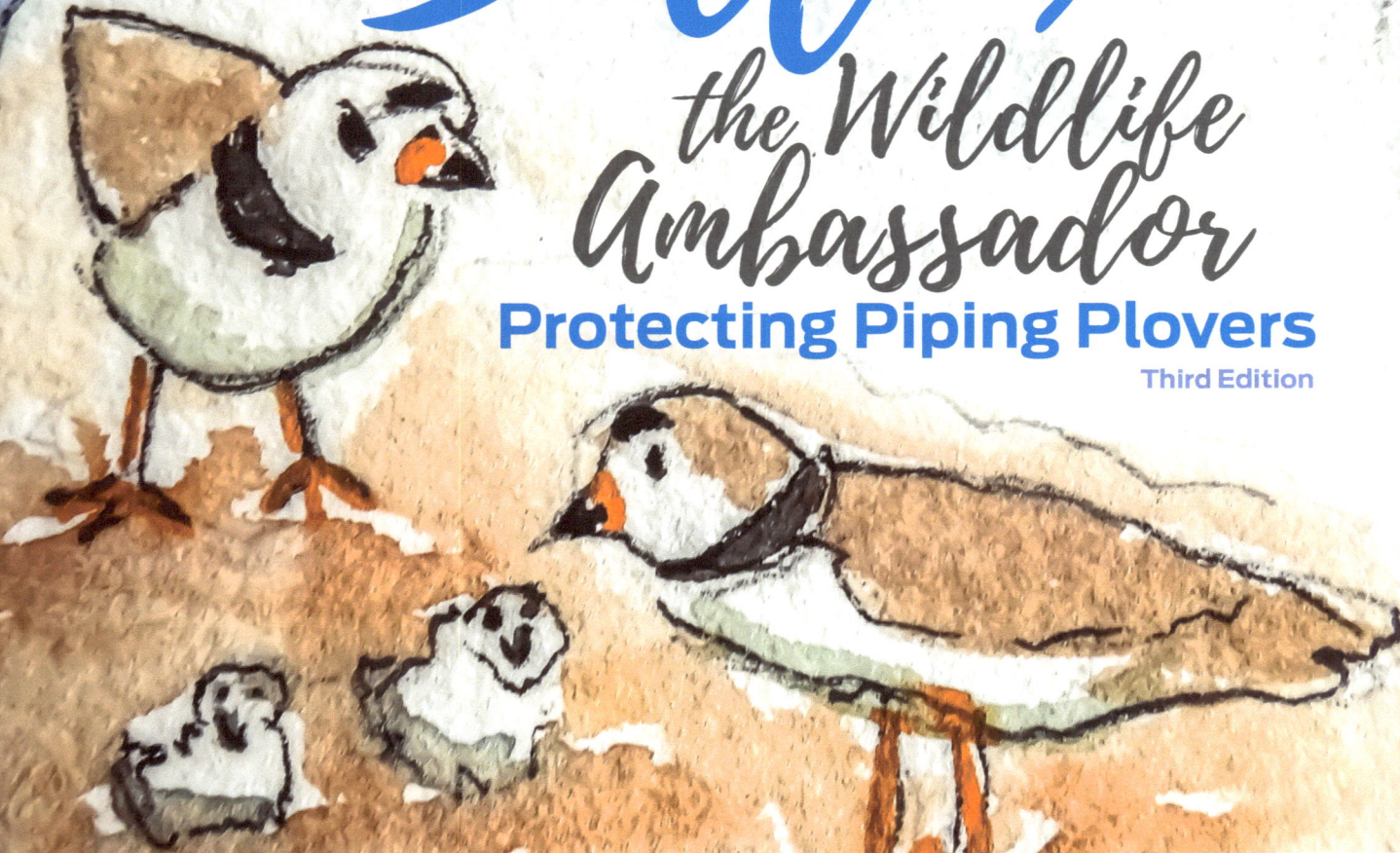

*The **Bella, the Wildlife Ambassador Series** is for families to read together and for dog owners who want to be responsible, informed conservationists. In real life, dogs and Piping Plovers do not mix. Turn the page to learn more about how to help these tiny, beautiful shorebirds, who face danger from a multitude of predators, displacement by human recreation and beach development, and disturbance by people and pets.*

Bella, the Wildlife Ambassador

Protecting Piping Plovers

By Katie Dolan & Judith Oksner

Photo credits:

Katie Dolan: page 14, 25, 26, 39, 41, 43-47

ISBN: 9781733958622

Hello. I'm Bella, a nine-year-old black Newfoundland. I recently retired from a journalism career at several fine publications, including BONE APPETIT, DOGUE FASHIONS, and DOG'S DIGEST. I wrote many words about the pros and cons of raw dog food, organic biscuits, and designer dog collars, but now I want to help wildlife. My human, Katie, and I often discuss the loss of animal species and the daily battles between people, pets, and wild creatures. As the world gets crowded with so many humans, cats, and dogs, our wildlife cousins feel the pinch. Wild creatures have nowhere that feels safe.

Katie's Notes: Wildlife Woes and Wins

- The planet's mix of species is rapidly changing due to habitat loss, pollution, introduction of animal species that do not belong in a new place, overhunting, overfishing, and climate change.

- A recent report finds the populations of vertebrates (animals with backbones) declined by 60 percent on average over the past forty years. Whale sharks, rhinos, forest elephants, and Great Apes are among the too many species that have suffered major population losses. Shorebirds are also declining.

- Of an estimated 8 million animal and plant species (75% of which are insects), around 1 million are threatened with extinction in the next few decades due to climate change, pollution, land use changes, and overharvesting.

- A detailed report on the status of Canadian and American birds finds that we have lost 3 billion birds since 1970. The major reasons for the decline are land use changes; pesticides, and predation by cats. Scientists conclude, "nature is unravelling."

- Humans throw natural balances further out of whack when they kill wildlife for food, sport, or to reduce agricultural losses. (Wild animals are often viewed as pests that eat grain crops or kill cattle or goats).

- In developed urban and suburban areas, adaptable wildlife species like coyotes and raccoons find plenty of food and their numbers are increasing.

- There are many potential ways for humans, pets, and wildlife to tangle with each other: the entire area of study is called "human-wildlife conflict."

- Despite these gloomy numbers, conservation can make a difference. Tiger and jaguar numbers have increased in key protected areas. Several species, including Black-footed ferrets and Kihansi spray toads, have even been successfully re-introduced to the wild.

- In addition, Humpback whales appear to be on the rebound around the globe, thanks to international protection agreements. The same turnaround is true for greater adjutant storks, American bison, and jaguars. Some waterfowl species are doing well, including ducks and geese.

It's the perfect assignment for me — a savvy Newfoundland Ambassador with a strong support team. Katie can easily find scientific information: she is a nerd who reads five or six books simultaneously. My handsome son, Blue, is an affable sidekick. Blue and I are members of a breed known for its giant size and gentle temperament. Fellow Newfoundland dogs have befriended baby birds and rescued rabbits. We'd never pick a fight with another creature — except maybe a cat. We can move quickly, especially when running towards someone offering a nice liver treat.

We are also great swimmers — it's in our genes. Our ancestors helped cod fishermen pull in heavy nets in the cold North Atlantic seas by swimming out to a buoy, grabbing it, and bringing it back to the boat. Newfoundland dogs are also expert water rescuers and were often stationed at lighthouses. One ancestor even rescued Napoleon Bonaparte when a large wave knocked the General into the water near the island of Elba. A Newfoundland named Plato was John James Audubon's canine assistant, retrieving birds for his master in Florida to identify new avian species.

A Newfoundland's double layered coat traps air and makes us buoyant. A unique frog-kick swimming style and webbed feet power us through the water. We are fast swimmers, although certainly not as fast as a polar bear, who can swim six miles an hour for days on end. This great swimming ability may be useful if we need to talk with sea creatures during our ambassadorial assignments.

Once my three-creature team decided to tackle the conflicts between wildlife, people, and domesticated pets, our first job appeared right in our backyard in Little Compton, Rhode Island. We live near a long stretch of beach that includes a town beach and Goosewing Nature Preserve.

All summer, beachgoers unload coolers, boogie boards, and plastic chairs to play in the shallow swells. They also enjoy the delicious hotdog stand. I love visiting that hotdog stand, too!

8

Little
mpton

Shaw

grand
Chace Pt.

Briggs Beach

Butts Rock

GOOSE WING

Past the last parking spot on the gravel causeway between beach and pond, the sandy shoreline extends for a mile long, curving gently towards a distant rocky point. Two shallow salt ponds lie behind the beach and dunes. The Nature Conservancy, wanting to protect the Piping Plovers (*Charadrius melodus*) and other creatures living in the salt marsh and on the remote beach, purchased the property many years ago.

By early September each year, Goosewing Beach has few people, but plenty of wildlife. On the pond, white swans imported from Europe reign like displaced royalty living in a foreign country. As the swans fly in mini-squadrons from pond to pond, their wings make a haunting sound. Ocean waves race towards the shore: sometimes powerful, blue-green combers roll in like soldiers in an orderly progression. On other days, the waves travel haphazardly, tumbling into one another like clumsy Newfoundland puppies.

The water in the inlet is still September-warm as Blue and I wade in the shallows. A thin great blue heron, almost invisible against the colorless ripples of water, flaps off screeching, "Go away, fat four-foots." A blue crab scuttles from the sandy flats into the submerged seaweed in deeper water. His gruff "What the heck?" is muffled by the rippling water and wind. We chase him, enjoying being the real kings of the pond. We are careful, however, to stay far away from the grumpy, hissing swans.

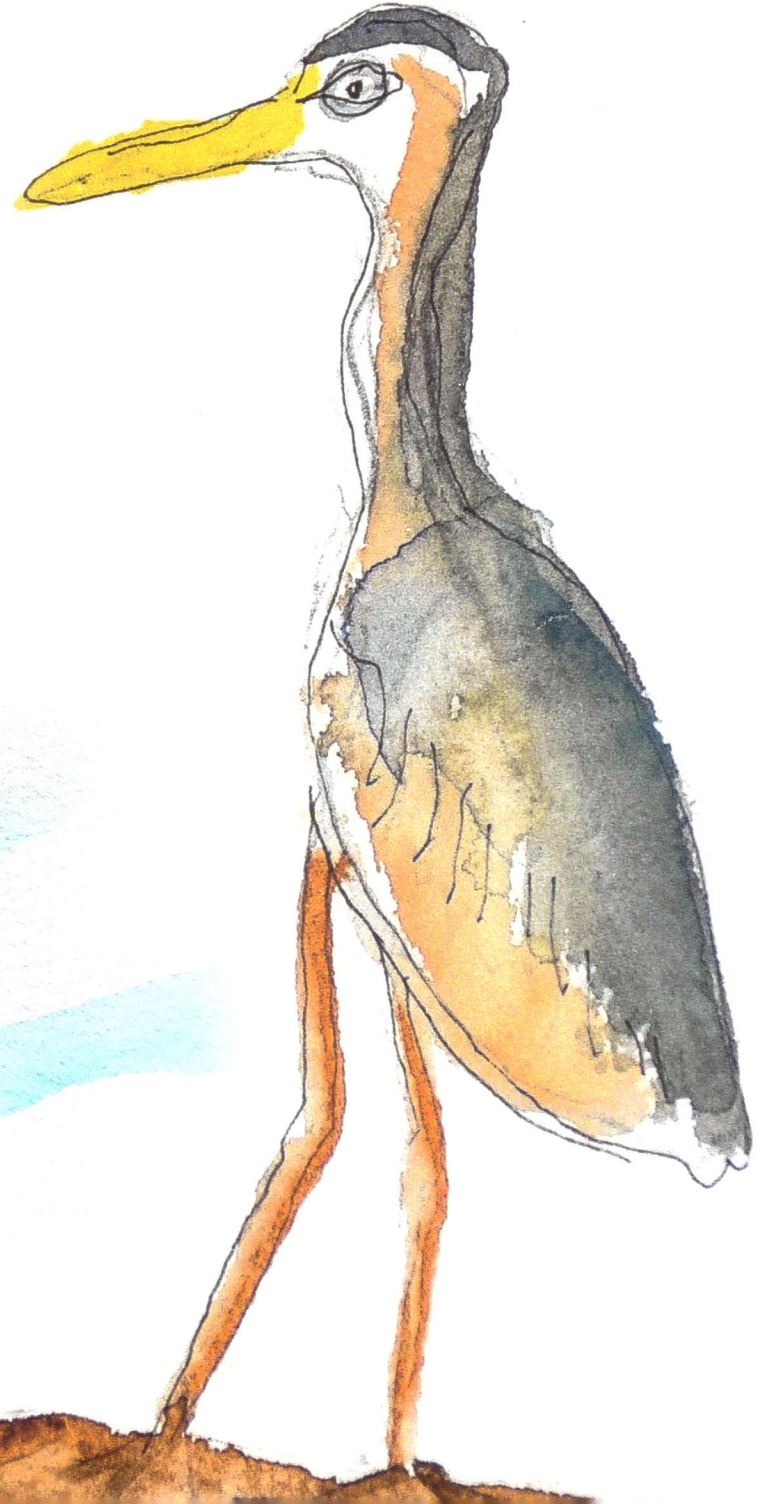

The thrill of the chase brings out strong predatory impulses, especially in a young dog like Blue. A few weeks ago, he saw something in the salt pond and sprinted over to investigate. He barked furiously, even more loudly than his everyday loud bark. He yelled, "Look, look, the water is swirling around like a flushing toilet. What is it? What is it? Come quick." I joined Blue, barking at the churning whirlpool in the otherwise quiet pond. I would have loved to get closer, but Katie reacted too quickly and snapped a leash on me.

She screamed, "No. NO. NO." and tried to wrangle Blue away from the whirlpool. But Blue is quick and strong, especially when he's excited. He splashed through the shallow water, barking. Another beach walker came over and the two humans finally put a leash on Blue. My strong son pulled and pulled, but they managed to drag him to the car. Turned out that all the swirling water was two snapping turtles mating in a frenzy of watery baby turtle-making. Thank goodness they had paid no attention to Blue. An angry snapping turtle — with its powerful jaws and sharp beak — could easily have broken Blue's leg.

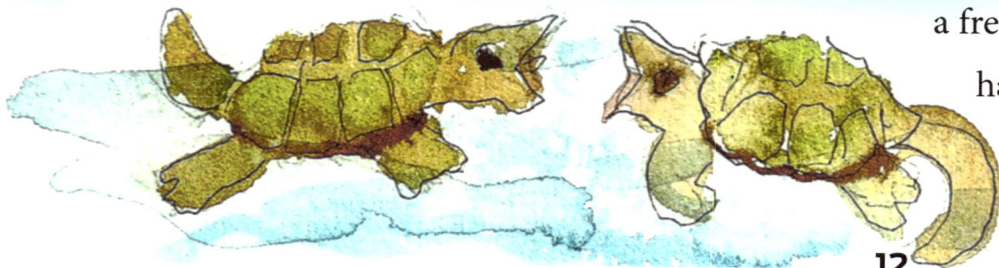

Speaking of legs and predators, I need to explain the Piping Plover rules of summer. Between April and September, dogs are not allowed to walk on Goosewing Beach because the tiny birds nest in the beach's dunes and cobblestone-filled sandy washes. These small, stocky shorebirds have a sand-colored upper body, a white underside, and orange legs. During the breeding season, the adults have a black forehead, a black neckline, and an orange bill.

Katie's Notes: Dogs on Beaches

- Dogs and piping plovers should not mix in real life, as the tiny birds scare more easily when they see a four-footed creature. In addition, the small chicks do not stay in the nest areas: they run all over the beach foraging for food and can easily be stepped on by a dog.

- In Gloucester, Massachusetts, dogs are banned from nesting beaches with heavy fines imposed. It's not enough to keep dogs leashed; they need to stay off plover beaches during the nesting season.

- Conservationists recommend that pet owners take the BARK pledge:
  B= Bag waste
  A= Always leash on plover beaches
  R= Respect wildlife,
  K= Know which beaches permit dogs

Picture taken in late October after the plovers have headed south. And, the dogs are both leashed.

They are very skittery little birds; the silhouette of a four-footed dog makes them even more nervous than the upright figure of a human. Perhaps plovers prefer creatures like themselves who walk on only two legs? Blue and I are happy to leave the plovers nesting in peace and to explore the adjacent town beach early in the morning before the lifeguards, sun worshipers, and swimmers arrive.

RESTRICTED AREA
PIPING PLOVER BREEDING GROUND

15

Since the plover nesting season is over, we can now explore the beach's far reaches. Suddenly, I hear a faint "peep, peep." The call gets louder as we approach the dunes. The Piping Plovers should have all headed south by now, but it's definitely a plover. I see a fluffy shorebird with a small, blunt beak like a stubby pencil that needs sharpening. It is perfectly camouflaged, blending into the backdrop of white and brown stones and shells.

I trot toward the tiny puff of plover. I stop twenty feet away and whisper, "Hey, little one. How are you?" The tiny bird says something, but too softly for my old ears to catch.

"Can I come a little closer?" I ask in a gentle, indoor voice.

"I've been running and flying from foxes and coyotes all day. I'm tired and think one of my wing feathers may be damaged," the bird peeps wearily.

"I'm not a fox. I'm a noble Newfoundland and will not hurt you," I say.

I explain in detail about the venerable, distinguished Newfoundland breed and my new role as a self-appointed Wildlife Ambassador. The little bird looks sleepy and a little bored, frozen in place. (Maybe I'll offer a shorter version of my pedigree next time.)

I lie on the sand nearby and wait, nonchalantly licking my front paws and pretending not to notice as the baby plover skitters closer. Finally, I ask, "What's your name, little bird?"

"Hercules. I was the runt of the second clutch, but my mother said I'd grow into my name. But, I can't gain enough weight if I'm running from scary things all day long."

"Well, Hercules, maybe you need a little snooze first, then you can tell us all about your busy, tiring day. Blue and I are expert snoozers. We'll show you how to relax on the beach. We'll be your sentries," I promise.

With that, Hercules closes his eyes and falls asleep. Blue circles a few times and then flops down nearby. I put my head down and we all rest.

In real life, conservation staff, who regularly monitor the piping plovers, would know a fledgling had not yet departed and might keep the dog restriction signs in place.

20

When Hercules awakes, he describes his little life, so far. "My parents had to abandon the clutch of eggs they'd laid earlier this summer because of the foxes. They moved down the beach to lay a second group of four eggs. This time, they picked a better nest site. Some loud, brave Least Terns nested nearby; they'd dive bomb potential predators, so we were all protected. My three brothers — Achilles, Odysseus, and Piper — were born twenty-seven days later."

Least Tern

"It's tricky finding a nesting site because beaches today are often crowded with people. Some of my cousins decided to nest in a narrow strip of vegetation in the parking lot of another Rhode Island beach. The local policemen erected barriers, so no one could park near the nest. When those chicks hatched, they made their way down to the beach on a specially prepared walkway with sand covering the hot asphalt," Hercules adds.

"Back here on Goosewing, my parents incubated us when we were mere eggs, carefully trading positions on the nest to keep us eggs warm. After we hatched, Mom and Dad took turns sitting on the nestlings. We'd snuggle into their bellies." At the memory of his warm home nest and of what he'd lost, Hercules sighs.

The little bird continues. "Soon after we hatched, we started to forage for tiny marine creatures in the moist sands on an outgoing tide. I stayed close to my brothers and parents at the edges of the beach near the waves. I learned the "foot-tremble" method where I stomp my feet and the movement makes our prey move and become conspicuous. I learned to listen to my parents' warning calls when people and other predators approached. If we saw a four-legged creature trotting towards us, my brother and I made a run for the nest. Mom feigned an injury, pretending her wing was broken. She'd drag her wing through the sand and hop around, distracting the intruder away from our nest."

23

"In the past few weeks, I've learned to fly, a bit. But, I wasn't ready to go when my brothers flew south a week ago. I'm not strong enough. It's been terrible being by myself. This morning, I was almost stepped on by a jogger fiddling with earbuds for his music and not paying attention to where he was running. Then, I had to hide from a circling raven… And the nights are worse. I hear prowling coyotes nearby and hide from the raccoons. I listen to creatures feasting on the garbage left next to the campsites. I worry every moment of every day and night."

The poor little bird sighs again. I worry that he's well on his way to full blown PTSD: Plover Traumatic Stress Disorder. Blue and I need to help. I bark, "Blue, I want you to stay here with Hercules and keep him safe. You are big; the foxes and other creatures will leave him alone." I go home, take a quick snooze, and wake up refreshed and ready to review the materials Katie pulled together.

Katie's Notes on Piping Plovers

- A Piping plover hatchling weighs only 1/5 of an ounce, which is the same as 2 pennies. In contrast, Bella and Blue weigh 140 pounds!

- Plover numbers fluctuate from year to year and are influenced by weather and the number of people on the beaches. During World War Two, gas rationing made it difficult for people to travel for beach excursions and so the plover population rebounded.

- Runoff in the Great Lakes led to record lake levels in 2019; the eggs from nests that would have flooded were taken to the Detroit Zoo to be raised/released.

- Hurricane-related surges and waves clear vegetation and create more nesting areas for the birds. Plovers have recently been doing well on Fire Island and there has been a 93% increase in their numbers.

- Although breeding pairs may return to the same beach together, juveniles usually disperse and do not nest on the beaches where they were born.

- Piping Plovers are one of many land/sea creatures and native plants specifically adapted to life on Atlantic beaches. The presence of Piping Plovers on a New England beach is a sure sign of health and ecological sustainability. Conservation groups and agencies charged with protecting nature choose to manage these beaches for Piping Plovers, knowing that if the Plovers are safe, these other creatures and habitat will endure, too.

- A folk song's refrain nicely sums up the many challenges: "Piping Plover babies are so small, people have to help them, or we won't have any Piping Plovers at all."

Katie's Notes on Shorebirds

- Millions of plovers, Least Terns, and other shorebirds were killed for their plumage to decorate ladies' hats in the early 1900s. Often, just the feathers were used, but sometimes several stuffed birds adorned a hat. The plume hunters' greed and women's fashions, combined with habitat loss and plover recipes, drastically reduced shorebird populations.

- New research suggests increased predation, especially in the Arctic and other northern breeding locations, is reducing the number of successful fledges of American Golden Plovers. Climate change appears to affect the mix of predators and their food choices so that more bird eggs are being eaten.

- As a result, shorebirds are one of the most threatened bird families in the world: only 2,000 piping plover pairs live on the entire Atlantic coastline. No one knows exactly how many plovers used to fly between their northern breeding grounds in New England, Canada, and the Great Lakes and their wintering grounds in the southeastern states, the Caribbean, and the Bahamas, but now they struggle to survive on remote beaches.

- Volunteers and staff from conservation organizations count the nests and chicks. They remind beachgoers to leave their dogs at home, stay away from nest sites, and smooth out the beach so little chicks don't get trapped in the holes.

It's a sad history for Piping Plovers, Least Terns, and their avian — bird — cousins. I must do my part to help Hercules and his brethren. I'll talk with my canid (dog family) cousins and other creatures to persuade them to leave the plovers in peace. Later that afternoon, I walk slowly around the large clump of beach rose bushes near the beach, sniffing out a fox den on the edge between the short grass and the large bushes. The foxes will just be waking up and I don't want them to be afraid or grumpy.

"Ahhhhhhmmmm…," I say, clearing my throat.

"Good afternoon. Do you have a minute, Mrs. Fox?"

"Good afternoon," she replies from inside the den. "Wait a minute while I wake the kits."

Mrs. Fox emerges from the den and nods a greeting. "My name is Vivian … Vivian Vixen," she says. Soon, five young red foxes tumble from the den. The kits, born in May, are as big as their mother. The youngsters chase each other, snapping at tails and baring pointed teeth. They are sleek and fast. They've fought vicious battles to establish a sibling pecking order and are more aggressive than my pups were at a similar age. They are definitely not gentle Newfs.

27

"**You've got some** fine kits there. I'm wondering what they have been eating? They are so big and strong," I say.

"Well, thank you," Vivian replies. "We eat a bit of this and a bit of that. My husband and I brought them rodents until the strawberries ripened and then we let them figure it out for themselves. A varied diet: mice, berries, bugs, grasses, squirrels, rabbits, mice, crickets, caterpillars, grasshoppers — you know, the Omnivores' Dilemma. On Sunday nights, we usually feast on beach garbage. It's so tasty, so varied. Hot dogs, clams, rolls, and corn cobs," Vivian explains, smacking her lips just thinking about the culinary bounty.

28

"Love those corncobs myself," I confess. "And, the smell of campfires in the dunes. Sometimes, I'll sniff out a half-eaten burger or a marshmallow that fell out of a S'more. Last summer, I gobbled four corncobs down. It was delicious, but then I had a giant stomach ache. I ended up in the Tufts Veterinary Hospital getting my belly shaved before emergency surgery. The cobs had become stuck, you see, in my stomach."

"Poor you. That must have been terrible," Vivian says kindly.

"But, let's get back to your food choices," I say. "What would happen if you didn't find human garbage down here on the beach?"

"*I'd probably* go back up and try near the farmhouse. I'd move the den up there, at the far corner of our territory. There are often nice food surprises. We eat whatever is nearby."

"What about shore birds?" I ask.

"Well, I've been known to taste a plover egg or two. You wouldn't believe what happened earlier this season. I went down to look — just to look — at the closest plover nest. It was enclosed by fencing. I crept closer, because I couldn't yet smell plover. I smelled food, though. It was odd. I went right up next to the fence. I must have brushed it with my whiskers and the tip of my nose. ZAP! A sharp pain and a tingly feeling up and down my snout. I screeched, jumped back, then yipped to the kits to follow me."

"Ah... Yes, I have heard about this. Katie, my human and research assistant, described experimental dummy nests with electrified fencing to teach predators to stay away from the plovers. But, instead of getting zapped, maybe a better solution is for you to eat and forage elsewhere. If there were less garbage left around, would you stay away from the beach? Would you find food in the fields instead? Could you give the plovers a chance?"

Vivian thinks a minute and says, "Well, yes, if you can get the coyotes, grey foxes, raccoons, crows, and cats to also agree to stay away from the beach. We generally compete for the same foods and we all love a nice morsel of baby bird. You'll need to keep the other animals away from the shorebirds."

I bid farewell to the fox family and trot down to the nearby beach. Relieving Blue of his bird-sitting duties, I settle down next to Hercules for the night shift. As I fall asleep next to the little bird, I form my ambassadorial plan. Blue and I will talk to the animals. I'll ask Katie to be a good nerd and research the complex relationships between predators. I'll get Katie to speak to the Town Council about higher fines for beach garbage and

education about the plovers. I think of a perfect, inclusive slogan: "People, Predators, Pets, and Piping Plovers: we're all connected." It's important to provide space and food for all creatures, not just humans.

Along with staff from local conservation organizations, Katie explains the shorebirds' plight and displays my slogan at the Town Council meeting. Soon a resolution is passed to increase littering fines and to hire more staff to pick up beach garbage. The Council also agrees to consider a new law requiring pet cats to be kept inside.

People, predators, pets, and Piping Plovers: we're all connected!

Katie's Notes on Predators and Mesopredators

- Apex predators—wolves, bears, and other large carnivores – keep everything in balance and ensure that there are not too many of one species or too little of another. They help control the numbers of smaller prey animals in an intricate, beautiful natural food web.

- Bears, cougars, tigers, and other large predators are frequently in conflict with humans because they will also sometimes eat sheep and cattle.

- When the apex predators disappear from a specific area (due to overhunting or being eliminated because they are considered dangerous to livestock), mid-sized mammals such as foxes and coyotes thrive.

- These "mesopredators" are good at adapting to people because they have small home ranges, a wide palate of food interests, and varied behaviors. Grey foxes are smaller and tend to live in wooded areas; they are the only canid (dog) species that can climb trees. Coyotes eat foxes, so more coyotes mean fewer foxes.

- Although hunted for their fur or killed because they are considered pests, foxes are also doing well because they reproduce rapidly (an average of 4 kits per litter). Foxes are more numerous than coyotes. Researchers know this by conducting scent station surveys, where they put out smelly bait to attract hungry animals and then count the number of wildlife prints or tracks the next morning.

- A healthy mix of wildlife keeps the ecosystem in balance and even helps reduce the number of ticks infected with Lyme disease. Possums and other smaller mammals groom and eat the ticks off their own bodies, so there are fewer ticks in the woods. A recent study found that one possum can eat 5,000 ticks each year! This result is a very good thing for dogs, people, and wildlife.

The next morning, Blue and I divide up the ambassadorial duties. We'll talk to the other animals: the cats as well as the coyotes, skunks and raccoons. We'll let them know the humans will leave less garbage on the beach. Goosewing will be less attractive for the predators.

"Let's not forget about the cats," Blue says. "I'll volunteer to talk with them. Please, please!"

"Blue, I know you. You want to chase cats, not converse with them. It's better that I go instead."

As I trot down the road to the neighborhood cat hangout, I think about cats and dogs as they relate to wildlife and my ambassadorial role. In my head, I make a chart. As you'd expect, dogs are not perfect but are clearly better than felines. Cats don't do anything good for wildlife, as far as I can see.

I arrive at Bass Drive, where the neighborhood's large Head Cat likes to sleep in the sun on a wide pergola beam. A pergola, by the way, is a series of wooden beams with spaces in-between that create partial shade on an outside porch. As I approach, the ginger colored tabby is in his usual spot atop the beam. A smaller white cat lies nearby. The tabby opens one eye and stares at me.

33

"Good afternoon, Cats." I say politely.

"Where's your loud, wild son? Is he hiding behind a beach rose bush?" The Head Cat says.

I laugh and answer, "No. I left him at home. Listen, we have something important to discuss, dog to cat." The Head Cat yawns, stretches, and stares.

"Okay. I'm waiting," he says.

"I'm here about the plovers. They've just had another poor nesting year and I'm worried that soon the beach will no longer have any shorebirds."

The Cat is silent. He washes his face with his paw, then says, "Yeah, they taste a bit like chicken."

"Well, here's the problem. Some of your cat clan kill birds not to eat, but merely for the sport of it," I say.

"Yeah, like some people we know," he says grumpily.

"Okay, let's not get distracted by the things humans do to make it worse for wildlife. I'm here to talk about problem cats. There's a trio of cats who've each killed more than sixty birds this summer alone."

"Yes, mighty fine hunters, they are," the Cat says.

34

"**Do you think** we could convince the three offenders to cut back on evening forays? And stop going down to the beach?" I persist.

"Ahhh… why would they do that?" The Cat asks suspiciously.

The smaller white cat lifts his head, looks at the ginger cat, and says, "You know, that trio is out of control. They kill for no reason, they bother other cats, and they say bad things about your leadership as Head Cat. I think they need to be put in their place. Show' em who's boss, Boss."

I add, "Could you persuade them? They respect you and, if you tell them to stop eating plovers, they'll do what you say."

The ginger cat nods in agreement and finally says, "I'll see what I can do."

"And I'll make sure that Blue leaves you alone," I add.

"It's a deal," says the Head Cat.

Dogs Versus Cats

Wildlife Pros and Cons: Bella's Canine Views

DOGS: There are an estimated 1 billion dogs on Earth. This includes owned, free-ranging, and feral dogs.

PROS:

- On South Georgia Island near Antarctica, rat-detecting dogs have saved the seabirds who nest there by sniffing out all of the rodents.

- In Patagonia, sheep dogs protect flocks from southern big cats like civets and cougars. As a result, the herders leave the wild cats in peace and do not kill them. Similarly, dogs often protect domesticated farm animals from wolves and cougars.

- Conservation sniffing dogs track scat to determine how many moose have returned to the Adirondacks.

CONS:

- Dogs, especially free-ranging ones that do not get veterinary care, spread rabies and other diseases to humans and wildlife.

- Dogs hunt and kill a wide range of species, including antelope, iguanas, kiwis, hyenas and civets.

CATS: There are an estimated 750 million cats in the world. Many are feral (not owned by anyone) and live in cat colonies.

PROS:

- Cats kill rodents and have often traveled onboard ships around the world to control rats.

CONS:

- In the United States, cats kill more than a billion wild birds annually.

- Cats spread a wide range of diseases to humans and wildcats.

- Feral cats on islands have been responsible for fourteen percent of the global extinctions of birds, mammals, and reptiles.

- The Stephens Island Wren, for example, was one of only a few flightless songbirds. It had an olive-green back, a pale breast, and a scalloped fringe of feathers. A pregnant cat names Tibbles came ashore in 1894. Within a few short years of living on the same island with Tibble's progeny, all the small olive birds were gone. The species disappeared forever.

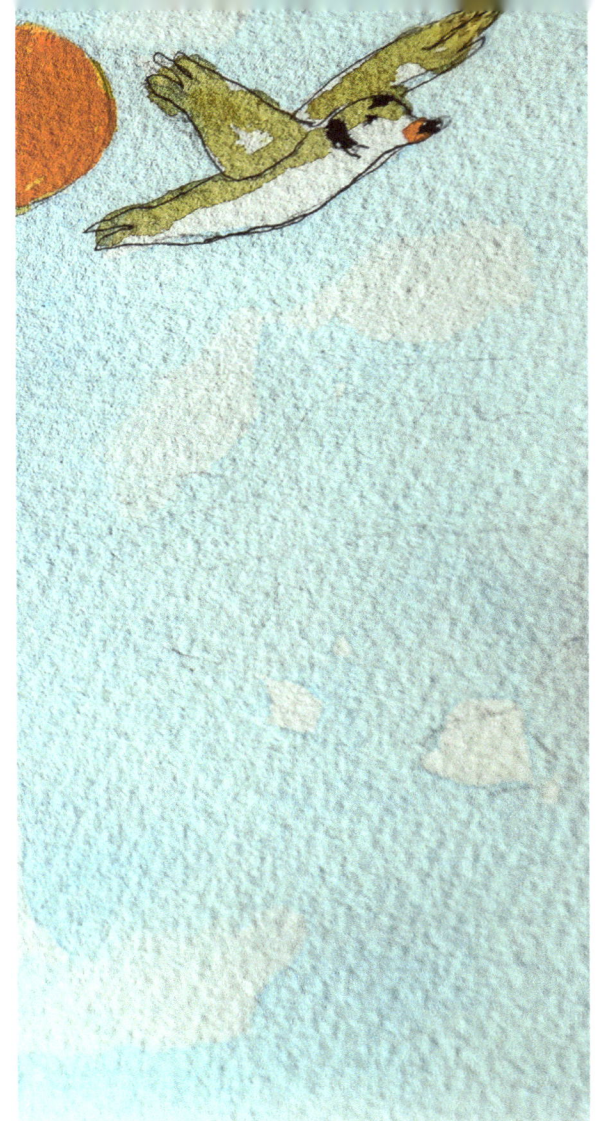

I trot back to Blue and we both walk down to the beach. Hercules is getting ready to join his siblings on warmer beaches. We tell him about our ambassador achievements and wish him well on his journey.

As we settle down to rest that evening, Katie says, "Listen to this — a great quote from Aldo Leopold, the respected naturalist. *"There are some who can live without wild things, and some who cannot."* It's sad to imagine a world with no wild things left.

I fall asleep, listening to Katie turning the pages of her book. I dream of seeing Hercules again next April. He'll tell us about his travels to the Bahamas or Georgia. He might be caught by researchers along the way and have bands and flags attached to his legs. Blue and I will tell him what's happened on Goosewing Beach while he's been down south. During the winter months, a dredging machine will cut a shallow channel, so the pond and its juvenile fish are reunited with the sea. The dredging will also create more of the moist, sandy habitat favored by Piping Plovers. In October, large boats trawling for giant sea clams will pepper the far horizon. Some of the bivalve catch will wash ashore and huge shells will litter the beach. These broken bits of white shell will help camouflage Hercules and his siblings next year when they return to the remote beaches of the Northeast.

Katies Notes: Bird Banding

- Some Piping Plovers are banded to show who banded the bird and where it was banded. If you see bands on a Piping Plover, go to www.fws.gov/ for details on how to report a sighting.

- The research shows that a Piping Plover pair will sometimes try to nest a mere 100 feet from a previous year's nest, even if the beach is no longer suitable for nesting because it has changed or is too busy.

- Other shorebirds, such as the American Oystercatcher, are banded and sightings of these birds should also be reported to help scientists understand how to protect them.

Hercules and his brave, resilient Piping Plover relatives will probably struggle again next year, but I hope some of my efforts will make a small difference for these small birds. As I roll over and take up a bit more space on the bed, I think ahead to my next ambassador job trying to help cougars and other wildlife in Colorado.

Katies Notes:
Help Bella Protect Plovers

- Don't leave garbage at the beach and be sure to follow the posted plover rules.

- Learn how to identify birds in your neighborhood. You can try Merlin, a cool, free app from the **Cornell Laboratory of Ornithology**, which analyzes a picture of a bird that is uploaded, makes a possible identification, and gives information about the species.

- Volunteer to help in the **Annual Christmas Bird** count by contacting your local Audubon Society Chapter.

- Go to Sci-Starter.org to see hundreds of projects where you can help scientists study wildlife by observing nature.

- Build a nest box for a bird species that might use your backyard.

- Keep your cat indoors.

- For additional information and resources on wildlife conservation issues, please visit Bella's Blog at katielangedolan-blog.tumblr.com

Katies Notes:
Pet Owners and Conservation

Pets are often major threats to wildlife, yet pet owners can also be important advocates for wild creatures.

- Pet owners are more likely to feel equalitarian with wild animals and to oppose hunting.

- Childhood pet ownership associated with adult concern for wild animals.

- Farmers who have pets show more positive attitudes towards large carnivores.

- A Norwegian study finds pet owners exhibit more favorable attitudes towards 24 different wild species; although both pet owners and non-pet owners had strong negative views towards rats, snails, beetles, and mosquitoes.

Find the Piping Plovers...

In the next four beach pictures, see if you can spot the Piping Plover.
Answers on page 47.

Answers

Resources

For Kids:

Krughoff, David. *The Endangered Piping Plover*

· Reigle, Janet. *Piping Plover Summer*

· Kim Smith Designs: A blog with great plover stories and pictures

For Adults:

Unnatural Companions: Rethinking Our Love of Pets in an Age of Wildlife Extinction by Peter Christie, 2020 pending publication by Island Press

The Seabird's Cry by Adam Nicholson

Cat Wars: The Devastating Consequences of a Cuddly Killer by Peter Marra and Chris Santella

Mountain Lion Foundation www.mountainlion.org